SEIZE WHAT

YOU SEE

How to Take Possession of
What You Dream and Envision

———

Dr. Kimberly Winters

SEIZE WHAT YOU SEE: How to Take Possession of What You Dream and Envision

Copyright © 2019 by Dr. Kimberly Winters

ISBN (978-0-578-57259-8)

DEDICATION

I dedicate this book to the One who gave me the words to express on every line and every page. He continues to show a Father's love for me in every way. I pray that I make Him proud in my obedience and use of the gifts that He has poured out upon me.

I want to dedicate this writing also to my handsome, devoted, wise, and most loving husband, Dr. Michael A. Winters. Without you, this book and so many other things would be left undone. You cheer me on, you love me relentlessly, you encourage me, and most of all, you inspire and empower me. You have taken every excuse away and pushed me to become a better woman in countless ways. I love you infinitely!

This book is also dedicated to my mother, Ms. Bobbie Adams, who is with Jesus. "Mama, I pray that I have made you proud in everything. I know that I have always been your "favorite daughter" just as my little sister, Tracy, has been. I love you all the way to heaven."

And finally, I dedicate this book to my children, Mychal and Victoria, who have been supportive and loving in all the seasons of our lives. I love you both. I pray that you both will walk into the fullness of what God has gifted you each to do. ONLY what you do for Christ will last. Be sweet!

ACKNOWLEDGEMENTS

Author Alex Haley once wisely said, "If you ever see a turtle on top of a fence post, you know that it had some help getting there."

As stated in this book, coaches and mentors are crucial for getting us to the next levels in our lives. There have been many influences in the past few years leading up to this book, but there are two that I will mention specifically.

Pastor Kimberly Jones has been my mentor and coach for several years and has called to life quite a few things I had no idea how to give birth to. I cannot put this book into your hands without a deep, heartfelt acknowledgment of her passionate influence on my life.

Mr. Felix Anderson has challenged my husband and I from the moment we encountered him. His outpouring of encouragement and desire to see others WIN inspired the topic of this book. He challenged me to "dominate my distractions" and "get this book into the hands of people who need it."

I am grateful for the inspiration and encouragement of my many family members and friends. It would require an entire, standalone book to name them all and to give proper "thank you's".

CONTENTS

FOREWORD

I can think of no other person more qualified to write the book that you currently hold in your hands. I have watched Dr. Kimberly Winters live and walk through the process that you will find outlined throughout this book. As her husband, I have witnessed firsthand how she has navigated the ebbs and flows of life. Kimberly exudes a confidence and a grace that only comes from knowing God through experiences in everyday living. She has encountered many hardships, setbacks, disappointments, victories, accomplishments, and successes. Her personal transformation has evolved through a relentless pursuit of running after the vision that God has given her when times were favorable and unfavorable. Regardless of which season of life, she has continually laid her life before God as a living sacrifice. I am blessed by my relationship with her and am a better man because of her impact. As you read this book, I encourage you to allow it to challenge your life and apply the action steps that are outlined to go to a new level on your own journey. The results will not only impact you but also those connected to you!

Michael A. Winters, Ph.D.

INTRODUCTION

There is generally a space between what we see and what we have. What we want or what we believe is for us, does not typically automatically become ours without some effort, even if only a minimal effort. To be clear as we begin, we are not referring to a new age philosophy of the law of attraction or anything of that nature. This is not that book. This book that you are reading is based on the understanding that God has shown you something that is for you or that He has given you a desire for something He wants you to have.

Imagine with me the scene of a parent holding an enticing object in front of a toddler who is learning to walk. The parent holds it up before the toddler believing that they will manage to wobble and get up on their tiny feet and take the three to four steps to get to the thing that makes their little eyes sparkle. As a parent, you would want your child to take the steps to *seize* what you wanted so badly to give them, but you also wanted them to exercise their little legs (faith) to receive it. That is how it is with God, our Father. He wants so desperately to give you the things you may feel are just out of your reach. He just wants you to desire it enough that you exercise your faith muscles to get up and seize it. He knows that in strengthening your faith, you will pursue the things He wants to give to you.

To seize means *to take eagerly and decisively.* It means to take possession of what you dream of and envision. The things that we dream of and envision come from God. Psalm 37:4 tells us that as we delight ourselves in the Lord, He gives us the desires of our hearts. I believe that as we delight in God, He *puts* the desires into our hearts for the things that He desires *for* us. By this I mean He causes us to want what He wants for us. This is not merely material things, though He does want to give us those as well. Our Father wants us to be healthy physically, emotionally, and mentally. He wants us to prosper financially so that we can provide for our own households, and to care for orphans, widows, the poor, and our local churches. He wants us to be blessed and to enjoy life abundantly. These are not selfish desires. Let's be clear. This furthers God's **kingdom vision** in the earth and in our lives.

A story from the Bible that comes to mind is the one about "Blind Bartimaeus," who called out to Jesus when he heard that Jesus was nearby. He called out despite the urgings of others for him to be quiet. When they told him to close his mouth, he shouted even louder. Jesus could not resist Bartimaeus' pleas for mercy. He beckoned for the blind man and immediately Bartimaeus, blind as he was, ran to Jesus. At that moment, Bartimaeus did not consult his legs and ask for their agreement. He got up on his feet and ran to Jesus! Jesus asked, "What do you want? What do you want Me to do for you?" As Bartimaeus reached out in faith for what Jesus held for him, Jesus gave him what he *dreamed of and envisioned.* Imagine that! A blind man with a **vision** and a dream to **see.** (Mark 10:46-52) Bartimaeus could not rely on what he saw with his natural sight, as he had none. He had to see from another place *beyond sight* to what it was that Jesus held for him. Too frequently we look to what we **see with our natural eyes** to inquire regarding what is not yet seen (spiritual) in the physical realm.

What is it that you dream of and envision? Looking into the distance at something that you desire and fully know is for you to obtain or achieve is fruitless unless you take some kind of action to bring it near. It is only when you take steps toward those things and extend your hand to grab them, that you can seize them. That same Jesus that held answers for "*Formerly* Blind Bartimaeus" holds the key for you. Seizing what you see is about positioning yourself for BIGGER things. You *must* see beyond what is in the realm of your current impossibilities and see the possibilities that God sees. Often, this means letting go of the familiar things and looking at and embracing things that seem way beyond your reach. If it was something that was attainable right now or did not require you to work and stretch to grasp it, it would not be worth seizing. You could already have it. You would not need an extended imagination or vision. Catch the revelation that you must SEE (vision) it to SEE (sight) it or you never will SEIZE it in reality.

CHAPTER ONE

---◆---

THE CHIEF ARCHITECT AND EXAMPLE: GOD'S IDEA FIRST

God is the Chief Architect and the example for us to seize what we dream of and envision. He is the originator of creativity. The book of Genesis tells us definitively that as God saw a thing, He spoke it into existence and it simply was. In this way, He created an entire universe that includes you and I. Ephesians 2:10 clearly tells us that "we are His workmanship (or masterpiece, as some translations state it), created in Christ Jesus for good works, which God prepared beforehand that we should walk in them." In Genesis 1:26-27, we read that God said, "Let us make human beings in Our image, to be like us...So God created...." We are made in the image and likeness of God and because He is creative, we are also creative. His nature is within us. We just need to tap into it for our own lives.

In order for any manufacturer, sculptor, artist, or designer to create or achieve any objective, they must first SEE it in their mind. They must form images of it COMPLETED through their imagination. No creator of any type just throws pieces, parts, or elements up into the air to just let things fall into place wherever they will. Thank God we do not have automobiles, airplanes, or homes assembled in this manner! No, they have seen the end of their creation and worked back from there to SEIZE WHAT THEY SAW, DREAMED, AND ENVISIONED. Homes and commercial properties are not created with whatever scrap building materials Lowe's, Home Depot, or the local building supply store has on hand. There was a blueprint involved that was carefully thought out and designed with the end in mind. Architects, contractors, builders, painters, and bricklayers all did their part to bring the projects to pass. God, being the Chief Architect, Builder, and example for us, put in us this same type of creativity and imagination for what we could see and seize.

What you are passionate about is usually a direct indication of what your purpose is. Those are things built into your DNA by God. What kinds of things make you happy and bring the most joy to you? What kinds of things cause you pain, sadness, and frustration? What makes you laugh? What ticks you off? These things point to and are clues to your purpose. Pray and ask God to show you the vision He has for you, more specifically, what your purpose is. The only way that you can seize what you see is to discover the purpose of it in your life and the congruence of it to your vision and life direction. In other words, does this make sense for my life? Will it enhance the vision I have for my life or will it take away from it? Then you must strategically plan and prepare to receive it. After this you must have a fervent pursuit and passionately lay hold of it, to SEIZE what you SEE. It will require patience and perseverance as you endure the process. You will need to be open to making godly partnerships as God links you to people who may hold the missing pieces to your mission.

Helen Keller, a deaf and blind author, educator, and activist, made this profound statement, "The only thing worse than being blind is having sight and no vision." We really cannot discuss seizing what you see without discussing vision. Vision is "the art of seeing what is invisible to others," according to Jonathan Swift. Vision is like gasoline in a car. It fuels your journey, your goals, and your mission. Without vision, you will not get very far and certainly not very rapidly.

If God has given us a vision of something to possess, He has also given us an authority to possess it. Bishop T.D. Jakes said that when he is presented an opportunity, he first asks the Lord, "Lord, is it mine? That's all I want to know, Lord, is it mine?" When he has gotten the assurance from God that it is his, he goes full steam ahead to claim possession of it.

How cruel it would be for someone to write you a check for $575,000 and then say that you cannot endorse the check and take it to the bank to cash it. If God has set it aside for you, He intends for you to have the authority to go to the bank to sign for it and claim it. He has given you the authority to seize what He has allowed you to see.

This reminds me of Isaiah 66:9, which speaks of the cruelty of allowing a woman to carry to full term to the point of delivery and then not being able to deliver what she has been carrying and nurturing internally. God is not cruel that way. He would not give you a dream and a vision of a thing so precious as what He has put in you, to allow you to nurture it and prepare for its arrival, just to say that it will not be delivered, revealed or brought to fruition. He is not waiting for you to arrive at this point just to say that He changed His mind at the last minute. I pray that you know He is much better than that and just like any Father waiting in great expectation for the "baby" to be born, He, too, is eagerly anticipating you giving birth to the thing He planted in you to carry and bring forth.

CHAPTER TWO

SHARPENING YOUR VISION

Many of us have some idea of what we want both short-term and long-term. Some of us have no clue at all what we should go after for our "now" or our "later." I call this sleepwalking. Sleepwalking through life can have deadly consequences. Accepting the days, weeks, and months as they come with no relevant plans and no subsequent actions is an unproductive existence. Having no vision is very dangerous and can be extremely costly to our futures. Proverbs 29:18 says, "Where there is no vision, the people perish: but he that keepeth the law, happy is he." The Message Bible puts it this way, "If people can't see what God is doing, they stumble all over themselves. But when they attend to what he reveals, they are most blessed." When we can see where God is leading us and then take the steps to walk it out, we will succeed. Joshua 1:8, "Study this Book of Instruction continually. Meditate on it day and night so you will be sure to obey everything written in it. Only then will you prosper and succeed in all you do."

How can we sharpen our vision? I am thrilled that you asked! First of all, as we have already established, we must HAVE a vision. When you lack wisdom and understanding, ask the One who gives wisdom liberally without judging you for lacking or for asking. Hopefully, it is crystal clear that you cannot see the best vision for your life without prayer. It is God who gives us purpose, as He knew who we would be before the foundations of the earth. Before we were formed in the womb, He knew us. Our purpose was established before we were ever a twinkle in our parents' eyes. Psalm 139:16 (NLT) says, "You saw me before I was born. Every day of my life was recorded in your book. Every moment was laid out before a single day had passed." How magnificent is that? That such an amazing Creator would think ahead through our purpose and put in us everything that we would need to accomplish what He already saw in us. As we search, we discover purpose and vision through the One who saw it before we would ever see it ourselves.

You can hardly resist considering the eagle when thinking about sharp vision. Eagles have what is called "binocular vision" just as humans, meaning they are able to keenly use both eyes simultaneously for excellent depth perception. But eagles have greater visual acuity from great distances as they fly high and swoop low to attack their prey. Eagles are fierce regarding what they see. They really go after it relentlessly. Spiritually, eagles represent an authority that we have. Their vision represents spiritual discernment and the clarity that is available to us.

From the eagle, we learn to 1) move to a higher vantage point so that you can see the broader picture; 2) be fierce regarding what you see and desire and; 3) walk in your authority which is granted by God.

Eagles have been known to throw their prey down from great heights and will not relent until the prey has submitted to their attack. They are very bold and calculating in their actions. They are dominant and confident. They fiercely seize what they see.

In my study of eagles, I ran across a piece of footage about eagles and how they will attack even large animals, often preying on mountain goats and other such large prey. They tackle whatever they desire. They are not inhibited or intimidated by the size of the thing that they see and want. Please catch that! The lesson here for us is that the size of the thing you see will not be an inhibition for you unless you allow it to be. I cannot imagine an eagle asking itself, "Hmmm, can I handle this mountain goat? Should I aim for a smaller meal and just be satisfied with that?" Let us bring their strategy for obtaining their meal into focus. They are very calculating and concise. When it is something that you know belongs to you, you find a way to obtain it, even if that way is contrary to the typical modus operandi for you. Ask God to stretch your imagination, to stretch your vision, to stretch your capacity to receive the things He wants to do in you and through you. You will only receive from God what you have the capacity to receive. Expand your capacity. DREAM BIGGER!

If we had even any indication of what God wanted us to want and to have, we would never settle for mediocre again. My husband is so colorful in his descriptions at times. He says, "God has an entire feast spread before us, but we're content to sit in the corner eating a bologna sandwich." Isaiah 55:8-9 paints a vivid picture that God's thoughts are not ours, nor are His ways our ways. The phrase "As high as the heavens are above the earth" describes how vastly different what we think and imagine are from how He thinks for us. We really must upgrade our thinking. Again, DREAM BIGGER!

Anyone can grab common things. It's God's desire for us to reach higher, stretch further, dig deeper into beyond what is presently obtainable for us. If it doesn't stretch you, challenge you, and scare you in many ways, you need to look again. When Elijah sent his servant to look at the sky and bring back a report of what he saw, each time the servant returned to Elijah with a report of nothing. "Look again!" Elijah said. Finally, after seven trips to observe the sky, he brought back the report of a cloud the size of a man's hand. It was the indicator of what was coming! If you are looking and what you see is too small, LOOK AGAIN until you can agree with God for the GREAT.

You can't seize anything until you see it. You can't see it until you *see* it. You must first see yourself laying hold of it before your hand can actually grasp it. Even in a natural, physical sense, there is an intrinsic function of eye-hand coordination. Even if your eyes are closed while grabbing for something, you are still seeing it in your mind. There is an undeniable connection between seeing or vision and seizing anything.

CHAPTER THREE

THAT'S NOT YOURS! DON'T PURSUE THINGS THAT DO NOT ALIGN WITH YOUR PURPOSE

Once you have your vision clear and understood, zoom in on the details and specific steps that must be taken to bring to pass what you see. This, of course, comes through trial and error and weeding out the things that do not feed your vision. Let's be clear, you must write the vision and make it plain so that you can run as you read it. (Habakkuk 2:2) You need to have your vision stated so clearly that a third grader can understand it. If it is overly complicated, keep working to simplify it. Simplify, simplify, simplify. This will often require a pruning or a cutting away. It can be extremely difficult to cut people and things out of your life that you have been connected to that require you to waste unnecessary time, trust me. Your vision depends on you making the tough decisions now so that you can run with this vision later. Most people really do not purposefully intend to take up so much of your time so needlessly. It simply happens before we or they even realize it. And unless we keep a tally of the minutes and hours as they quickly tick by each day, we can look up at 5:00 PM and have no accounting for where the time went.

It is one thing not to even try to pursue purpose at all, but to ignore it, to delay it, or to shrink back from it, is something else altogether. What happens if you pursue the wrong purpose or life goals? The result, either way, is likely going to be frustration, lack of fulfillment, and wasted time. I know you have seen little girls playing dress up and they have on their mother's dress, jewelry, shoes, and all the accouterments associated with this dress up game. When we try to walk in someone else's calling, their shoes, and their roles, we are essentially playing this same dress up game. When we try to adapt our lives around other people's expectations and dreams, their restrictions, if you will, we are like a square object being forced into a round hole. Pursue those things that align with your purpose. Allow me to tell you my own story of trying to adapt to something that obviously was not in alignment with what was intended for me.

After I had been practicing dentistry for several years and had been working for a number of those years as an associate dentist employed by another dentist, I decided I needed to try to get out on my own and open my own practice. My patient base was enough to sustain my own business at this point. In preparation for moving out, I found a small building with a vacant corner office space. It was literally a tiny corner! There were several other businesses there and the portion of the building that I would rent only had two rooms available, but I was willing to settle for that to change my then current situation. I got a business plan together, approached a banker at a small local bank for a loan to get started, and was squarely turned down. I had placed all my hopes in this venture and was looking forward to the chance to hang my own sign! He refused me, saying, "We would like to help you, but..." I was utterly devastated. The hope was dashed right out of me. Back to the drawing board and back to someone else's office.

I loathed the banker. Honestly, I stayed mad at him for years even though I was a Christian woman serving God. As shameful as that is, it is the truth. Yes, I repented to God, but I did not, in my limited mindset, recognize that this was the hand of God through this man. God was closing the door to something far smaller than what He wanted to bless me with and bless others through in my life and business endeavors. I have since that time confessed this to that banker and thanked him for being a vessel used by God to redirect me. He now welcomes my business!

Several years after the first let down, another opportunity was presented, this time for my own building on my own prime land. I rewrote my business plan for this new location and spoke with a different banker. This second banker did everything he could to help me and to give me "yeses" at every turn in the process of construction of my very own building. He too was a vessel of God in the right time for me to seize what I could see. Once I was in alignment with my purpose, the right circumstances opened up for me.

I certainly do not want to leave you with the impression that things will be perfect when they align with your purpose. However, there is such a greater level of contentment to be experienced when you know you are walking in the will of God and in alignment with what is yours.

CHAPTER FOUR

——— ❦ ———

WHY WE FAIL TO SEIZE WHAT
WE WANT TO SEE

Picture this: You plan a menu for a dinner party at your home for a few friends and family. In preparation to feed and entertain your guests, you head to the market to grab everything needed to make a delectable 5-course meal. After the trip there, the time it takes to find all the right items, and then the long wait in line, you get all your items bagged, in the car, and then into the house upon your return. You unpack and put away all the groceries and start your "mise en place" (pre-cooking preparation)—oh yes, it's fancy. You begin to cook, and you suddenly realize that some of the main ingredients that were necessary for this evening's dinner party were not purchased today. You cannot complete this meal until all these things are in place. Much the same way that this dinner party preparation cannot be completed until all the things are in place, you cannot walk into what is for you until you have everything in place. Not that every detail is perfect, but you must have certain things in position before you can even begin to grasp what you believe is yours.

What are the things that can stand in your way? What ingredients are missing? What are the things that oppose our grasping what God has for us? What obstacles or barriers do we have to overcome in order to seize what we see? These are different for every person and for every circumstance. This is certainly not an exhaustive list that I have assembled here, but let's take a glimpse into a few of the things that can hinder us. Perhaps reviewing the suggestions below will stimulate your recognition of the things that hinder you personally, then you can use the notes and action-steps pages at the end of this book or perhaps a journal, to add to your own list of things to confront.

1. Your mind. Faulty thinking can sabotage even the best-laid plans. You can desire to do one thing, but if your mind is not renewed your plans will fail. It will be like a war within yourself. You can have great intentions and big aspirations as a child to become a physician when you grow up, but because you have not renewed your mind to study and to pursue the path that leads to this career, you have only wished for it to be so. Far too many times we believe that "wishes come true", but the truth is that prayer and putting in the work are the only sustainable ways that these things come true.

Self-limiting thoughts can certainly work against your best potential. Henry Ford said, "Whether you think you can, or you think you can't, you're right." If you are constantly demeaning yourself, criticizing your abilities, counting your weaknesses, and expressing low esteem of yourself, you will see yourself at the bottom in every situation. You will never see yourself conquering in any event. One of my favorite pictures of this concept is in the Bible story of the spies being sent into the land flowing with milk and honey. Joshua and Caleb came back with a report of possibility, hope, and excitement about victory and the ability to possess what God promised them! They even brought back physical evidence to prove that what they saw was real; The hugest clusters of grapes they could imagine. It took two men to carry the grapes on a pole between them! They seized evidence of their coming reality. The others previously sent out, came back with the report of how small they were in their own eyes and presumably small in the eyes of the enemies. They saw themselves as small as "grasshoppers." They framed things differently in their minds and what they saw, they became. "Whether you think you can, or you think you can't, you're right."

Fear of failure and fear of success both can be paralyzing. They can hinder us in the most detrimental ways, causing us to hold back and to rethink or overthink every decision we try to make. Both, in their own manner, can keep you from reaching out to take possession of what you know you need and what God wants you to have. The Bible makes it quite clear that fear is a spirit. Realize that it does not come from God, but that He wants us to operate in power, love, and a sound mind. Perfect love, which comes from God

SEIZE WHAT YOU SEE

and IS God, casts out fear. (2 Timothy 1:7; 1 John 4:18; 1 John 4:7-8)

2. Team.   Surrounding yourself with the right people is so critical to achievement and success. There are things that on this current level you do not yet have the knowledge or skill to reach in order to get to the next. It is necessary to have people on board that not only encourage and stretch you but also can see beyond what you can see and imagine. Some of the wisest men and women I have ever heard speak and teach have said that their success was largely due in part to the fact that they surrounded themselves with people who were strong in their own particular areas of weakness. Realize that there are others who can see in your blind spots and can help you to navigate through those areas of weakness where you need to improve. Let me put a plug in for coaching here. Even the most highly skilled

athletes need great coaches to take them to the next elevation in their mastery. As skilled as the Williams sisters are in tennis, they have needed to change coaches over the years to take them to new levels. The coaches they have chosen, have had the ability to see their potential in ways they could not see for themselves, assisting them in becoming world champions in their sport. You need people who can recognize great potential in you and who can help you to dream and envision more than you are capable of on your own.

Regarding my own story of becoming a dentist, I could always see it, even when some others could not. I remember hearing the words, "Are you sure you want to do that? Why don't you try to do something else, something attainable for you?" "Do you know any black female dentists?" I even heard a dental school instructor tell a female classmate/friend of mine that "women are not cut out to be dentists." You see, there were many voices intentionally or unintentionally, directly or indirectly, that spoke negatively regarding my destiny, contrary to what I had seen for my future. If I had listened to those people, well-meaning and sincere as they may have been, there are many lives that would not have been impacted by my 25-year career as a dentist, including the lives of my own family.

Near the end of my senior year of college at Alcorn State University, I had to make a decision about my next steps. Among my choices were 1) to forge ahead to dental school as I had planned, 2) to go to graduate school, or 3) to teach biology somewhere. The cost of professional school was incredibly scary. I was from a single parent home and did not have a "rich uncle." This was my dream, but financing it terrified me. My aunt was frequently telling me to finish what I had started, and that I had come too far to stop now. Fortunately, I had a college professor who was "in the know", and she informed me about the various ways to get scholarships and loans even for professional school. Sure, I had a backup plan, but in my heart, I really did want to SEIZE WHAT I SAW! I wrote essays and placed applications with local organizations as well as national corporations who gave scholarships to students. One of those corporate scholarships was from the Colgate company and I was thrilled to receive their assistance toward my dental education.

Near the end of dental school, completing the requirements was very demanding and rigorous. It was a very physically, mentally, and emotionally challenging time for students. There were some who quit and many who thought about it. I was in the second group, thinking about it.

It is always crucial to know who you are surrounded by in times of adversity. I can recall vividly several of us sitting in the small call center where we called our patients. We were crying and griping to one another about how hard and nearly unbearable it was and how many procedures we still had to complete on our patients in order to graduate. I remember how we encouraged each other to make it through those last few weeks and through our national and state dental board exams. You know, if I was surrounded by quitters or those who did not want to see others win, this commentary could be very different. I wanted them to win and they wanted to see me win! Mindset is everything. There was no "You should just quit then" or "It was too hard for you anyway." No! I was surrounded by people who said, "You've come too far to turn around" and "You were made for this"!

3. Motivation vs. discipline. "I would get into the gym more if I could just find the motivation." "I would read and study more if I could just be more motivated." "I would start the business I have been thinking about if I could just find the motivation." Motivation is a reason or a strong feeling to do something. Discipline is doing something long after the motivation has passed. Discipline is staying in the gym because you know that the long-term benefits to your health outweigh your feelings about going to the gym at the moment. Motivation thinks about the "here and now", while discipline thinks about the days and the years to come. Discipline is sticking to your business plan and strategies you have put in place long after your excitement about opening the business has waned. Discipline is hanging in

there after the bills have begun to come and you are not taking an income home for yourself yet. It is planning the work and working the plan despite the current state of things. Discipline is studying and preparing for the opportunity of a lifetime to come because you know it will and "feelings" won't cut it. Motivation is your "why", while discipline is the self-governing method or system to fulfill your "why." When we drop off at motivation, we will never seize what we see, or possess what we dream of and envision.

It has been stated that it takes between twenty-one to thirty days to form a habit or to change a behavior. Considering this, what happens when one day you are not motivated to perform the new behavior and you revert to old habits? When discipline is the new normal, regardless of how you feel, you push past feelings and achieve what you intended. What a wonderful sense of accomplishment!

4. No pattern. When God shows you something or you dream of something that you have no visible pattern for, it can be difficult to wrap your mind around it and understand how materialization will occur. Just because it has never been done before is no reason to believe it cannot be done through you.

I have heard stories of world records being set, stories of new scientific discoveries being made, and all sorts of new and wonderful firsts in history. What if those who took those first steps allowed the words "it has never been done before" to frame their actions? We would have no modern medical cures, procedures, and techniques. We would be limited in innumerable areas. Clearly, it does not matter how large or how small your personal accomplishments are, break the mold!

When people have not seen a pattern or a model for something, they may try to convince you that you cannot do it either. Remember though that they are not always operating with malicious intent. They are just applying their limitations to your situations. They are putting you in the box of their limited exposure. "There are no miracles in the familiar (comfort zone)", says Bishop T.D. Jakes.

God has called me to be a trailblazer, going where no one in my close family has gone before me. He has called you to blaze some trails too. BE THE PATTERN. Do not just follow patterns.

5. Permission. Do you remember the games "Mother May I" and "Simon Says" from

childhood? Both of those games required permission from someone else before you could make a move or take the next steps or actions. In "Simon Says" you could do the action you were told to perform, but unless it was prefaced by "Simon Says" from the leader, it was an illegal action and you were disqualified. In "Mother May I", if you did not ask "Mother" for permission and you just did the actions, you were required to return to base as if you had never started.

Too many times we think we need the figurative "Mother's" or "Simon's" permission, approval, or acceptance before we can do what God has put in our sights to take hold of, or to seize. I understand that it is part of our nature to seek endorsement and affirmation that we are doing the right things. There is nothing wrong with you wanting validation. That is actually quite normal. However, allow me to challenge you here. Who decides that being normal in everything is a standard to live by? You were made to soar above average. You were created to be exceptional! You have the approval of heaven to do it.

CHAPTER FIVE

Seizing Opportunities

Once you have set your sights on what you envision, or what God has shown you, it is time to put a plan into action to take possession of it. Not every opportunity comes around a second, third, or fourth time. To be perfectly honest, though He will give us second chances, God does not owe you that chance when you have not followed through on the first opportunity. Leonard Ravenhill said, "The opportunity of a lifetime must be seized within the lifetime of the opportunity." I remember being in junior high school and smelling the fresh bread every day from the old Sunbeam bakery across the street. There was nothing like seeing our assistant principal, Mr. Henley, coming back into the building with that brown paper bag. He would come into the office and extend the open bag with a friendly offer of a pinch of hot bread out of the bag. Never turn down fresh, bakery-hot bread! Many people are crazy about the Krispy Kreme light coming on in that same way. If the light is on, they are stopping. These are just some of those opportunities that must be seized when the time is right. Never carelessly think that opportunities have no expiration date.

Let's revisit Ephesians 2:10. It tells us that we are God's masterpiece created for good works that we should walk in them. The Passion Translation puts it this way, "We have become his poetry, a re-created people that will fulfill the destiny he has given each of us, for we are joined to Jesus, the Anointed One. Even before we were born, God planned in advance our destiny and the good works we would do to fulfill it!" One thing we can be certain about in reading this is that we have good works to do.

So how do we go about getting this all in motion? Through a vehicle I like to call The P9 Process. It involves the following nine elements crucial for your success as you pursue what you have envisioned for your life.

Prayer: As a believer, absolutely nothing should begin apart from prayer. It should be the foundation of every facet of your life. It is where you and God meet and He is able to download the vision, the resources, the strategies, answers, and the means to accomplish the vision directly to you through the Holy Spirit. You can take on things on your own, but why would you do that? Our capacity is so limited without the Creator of the world setting the stage of your life and opening doors you never knew existed without

Him. Pray through every phase, committing every step of your achievements to Him.

Purpose: Discover what your good works are purposed for. What has God destined for you that is a unique life-design just for you? Dr. Myles Munroe said, "When purpose is not known, abuse is inevitable". You must begin by knowing your purpose and what the purpose is of the thing you see. You should know how it will work for your overall vision.

Plan: Strategize how to carry out what you are purposed for. We have already established that without vision, people perish. Now that you know the "what", it is vital to establish the "how." Without a plan, you only have a wish. Plans are what keep you from wandering aimlessly through your days, weeks, months, and years. Writing out a plan is laying out the sequence of steps that will ultimately bring you to what you see.

Prepare: Do the necessary work to get ready for the plan God has shown you. You have heard the expression a thousand and one times, "Stay ready so you don't have to get ready." It is such a powerful statement. Prepare for SUCCESS. Plans are the blueprints for building, but preparation is breaking up the ground and laying the foundation for building. Emerson said that "the future belongs to those who prepare for it." I want to ask you a serious question. Have you prepared for what you have prayed for? What good is it to receive answers to your prayers and you have made no preparation or provision to receive the manifestation of those answered prayers. No planter sows seeds without expecting a harvest from his planting. Because he expects what he plants to grow, he has a barn ready to receive the harvest. Prepare for what you pray for.

Pursuit: Once you have made the necessary preparations, now it is time to hit the proverbial pavement. Very rarely, if ever, do things just materialize without you putting in the work. Seek God fervently in prayer about which doors are your doors and then ENTER. Go after it. Do the work!

Passion: As you seize what you have seen, dreamed of, and envisioned, walk and work with passion and intentionality. Dreams are not meant to be breezed through without utilizing the senses that God gave you to feel the sand between your toes, to smell the ocean, to see gorgeous sunsets, to hear children laughing and playing...you get the picture. Enjoy the journey set before you!

Patience: We said nothing is automatic. We don't go to fitness centers once and leave buffed! It takes patience and perseverance.

Patience makes me think about my grandmother and the way she could cook. People STILL talk about her cooking today with great fondness! She would make these homemade yeast rolls that would make you slap somebody else's mama! The only things that remotely come close to my grandma's rolls are Sister Schubert's store-bought rolls in the round foil pan. I can remember her instructing me in making them at her house for holiday sales and a few for us. After a tedious process of mixing the dry ingredients, wet ingredients, and then all of it together, the dough had to be covered and left alone to rise. Then it had to be kneaded and left to rise a second time. You better not think this would be a brief process and that you would be enjoying these rolls quickly. However, whenever they were baked and it was time to enjoy a fresh, hot buttery pan of them, my, oh my! And homemade jelly or fruit preserves of some kind just added to the delight for our palates. Occasionally, she would tuck just a small bite of country ham inside each roll as she rolled them out. Patience has its rewards!

Perseverance: This is steady persistence in a course of action, direction, or path especially in the face of difficulties, obstacles, or discouragement. It means to not quit regardless of how difficult the road is to navigate. Mountains by their nature are difficult to climb, but there is a tremendous reward when you see the view upon reaching the top. When what you see does not line up with what you are believing for, this is not the time to quit. It is the time to dig your heels in much deeper and keep standing until what you are believing for and what you know is for you, comes to pass.

The point that I hope was conveyed to you through this book through practical understanding and through my testimonies is that seizing what you see, possessing what you dream of and envision is not necessarily an easy or automatic event. It requires a made-up mind, diligence, and confidence in God and the abilities He has given you. Then you have to put in the work to arrive there. Most things worth having do not come easily. It is going to require movement and change, growth and transformation. What does a life look like where a person fails to seize what they see? They most likely have lives of regret and remorse. Settling, stagnation, or always pondering "what if" ... That's no way to live. That's no real quality of life, or at least not the BEST quality of life. We have been promised an abundant life.

Partnership: None of us can do the things we do alone. We need partners in purpose to get the job done well. Our greatest partner is God. I have heard some entrepreneurs use the expression, "God is my CEO." I concur with that statement because when we attempt to conduct our affairs alone, without God, misery is often a byproduct. However, with Him leading, success is guaranteed. As we partner with Him, He adds His super- to our -natural and supernatural things are released and experienced.

People are answers to many problems that confront us. We are answers to many problems that confront other people. Do not resist to enter partnerships with other people that God connects you with. You could call a halt to the very solutions that you need to get to your next level.

CHAPTER SIX

Practical DOES IT

You may be wondering to yourself, "What does it look like to seize what I see in my everyday life? How do I apply all of this where I live?" I want to leave you with a very practical blueprint with which to begin, one that you can easily modify for your purpose and style.

First, you must identify what it is that you are to seize. Identify it and ask if it aligns with what God has shown you as the direction for your life. Does it add value to your life? Does it benefit your family and those you are connected to? Who else will it benefit from it? Think in terms of your community, your place of employment or your employees, or perhaps business partners. What cause will it advance? Will it serve kingdom vision or detract from it? This is not the time for distractions.

Next, ask how you can get it. What will it cost in money, time, or other resources? A wise person only builds after counting the cost. Also, remember that a God-sized vision is, or may be, beyond your present abilities or skill set, and will require His help attaining it or accomplishing it. "What special skills might be needed or am I capable of getting this done just with what God has given me for right now?" What obstacles stand in your path?

Thirdly, sustaining the dream and vision and reaching further beyond that will require you to be able to shift as God shifts. Do not get so attached to one way of functioning and implementation that you cannot adapt as life demands. God operates level to level, dimension to dimension, grace to grace, higher and greater. He operates in realms; not always linearly as we think. He remains the same, but His ways of doing things are subject to change.

God has no delight in our being content with where we are today. This is the reason He shows us the vision and then challenges us to seize it, so that we produce and advance. He could just give us everything He wants us to have, but that would not give us the impetus to stretch and grow.

Butterflies have always been quite interesting to me. In my studies, I have learned that if you break a butterfly out of its chrysalis too soon, it will die. You may think you are helping by speeding up the process so that it can fly sooner. However, it is the process of "breaking through" that forces fluid into the veins of its wings and gives it the strength to fly. It dies if it does not complete this metamorphosis by these means. Accept the process by which God has chosen to cause you to grow and mature. Strength is built through resistance.

Pray daily for clarity of vision for the will of God for your life. Write the vision. Do not count on your memory. Thoughts are fleeting due to the busyness of life; therefore, paper and pen are useful tools to keep near. Put it down and keep it before your eyes. Revise as needed.

Write and recite decrees and declarations that align with the word of God for your life. Job 22:28 (Amplified Version) says, "You will also decide and decree a thing, and it will be established for you; And the light [of God's favor] will shine upon your ways." Speak the word of

God about your life and vision. Mark 11:23 tells us to speak to the mountain for it to be lifted up and removed into the sea. There are many verses in the Bible that express to us that what we ask in Jesus' name, we have authority to receive. You have to know the word of God to apply it appropriately.

Show up daily in your own life and do the work. Walk it out. Commit to stop sleepwalking through your life. No one can live it for you and there is too much invested in you for you to ignore what God has shown you. He wants you to receive it and to live it out purposefully.

Do not miscalculate the intentions of the enemies of your vision. You will not necessarily go in and walk right out with the things you dreamed and envisioned in your hand. Most often you only gain the prize through a fight.

There is a reason it is called "prizefighting." One of the biggest untruths told is that when it is "right", it is easy. Some of the best, most rewarding triumphs have come after your greatest fights. Do not throw in the towel simply because it is hard in this moment.

Do not despise the process. Why do butterflies begin as caterpillars? They begin as such because there is something that they get through the process that they cannot get in any other way. The process makes them what they become. The same applies to you and I. The processes we go through, great or small, manageable or difficult, bearable or heartbreaking, all work together for our good. Romans 8:28 (New Living Translation) reminds us of this, "And we know that God causes everything to work together for the good of those who love God and are called according to his purpose for them."

Be obedient and true to what you know will lead you to the destination before you. With faith and determination, SEIZE WHAT YOU SEE.

Use your own journal or the next couple of pages to begin your process to SEIZE WHAT YOU SEE, TO POSSESS WHAT YOU DREAM AND ENVISION.

FINAL THOUGHTS

As much as I would like to leave you with the "warm and fuzzies" after reading this book, I feel an urgency for you, the reader, to get up and go get it. What is "it"? Whatever you have put off while waiting for a better day to come, hoping for someone else to get to it. You know, that thing that God has put on your mind over and over again, that thing he's been urging you to put your hands to, that task that you have looked the other way concerning. There will never be a right time if you are waiting on circumstances to be ideal. I hear people say regularly that they are waiting for their children to get out of school, or that they are waiting until they have all the money that they anticipate needing for that startup business.

Most often, God meets us "as we go." He told Abraham to get out of his father's house and go to a land that He would show him. Abraham had a promise from God that would certainly be fulfilled, but it was contingent upon Abraham's obedience. He had to go. James 4:8 tells us to draw near to God and He draws near to us. I believe that as we draw near to Him, He does not come empty handed. I believe that He meets us and, as Psalm 68:19 makes clear, He "daily loads us with benefits." There is a responsibility that comes on our part. When He presents you with the dream and vision, you cannot simply look the other way. We must SEIZE what we SEE and take possession of what we dream and envision!

CHAPTER SEVEN

Notes, Questions, Action Steps

Please take some time to think about and answer these questions and perhaps add some of your own. Starting a journal would be a magnificent idea. Writing the vision helps to make it plain. (Habakkuk 2:2-3)

What is it that you see?

_____

_____

_____

_____

_____

_____

_____

Are there things that hinder your vision of what God may be trying to show you?

_____

_____

_____

_____

_____

_____

Are there things that you may have allowed to hinder you from seizing what you dream of and envision?

_____

_____

_____

_____

_____

_____

How can you reposition yourself to seize these things now?

_____

_____

_____

_____

_____

_____

What things will you put in place going forward to be successful?

_____

_____

_____

_____

_____

_____

ABOUT THE AUTHOR

Dr. Kimberly Winters is by profession a general dentist and has been in practice for 25 years. She is an ordained minister of the Gospel, a certified professional life and empowerment coach, a conference host and speaker, a prolific teacher, and an author. She co-founded The Purposed Group with her husband, Dr. Michael Winters, and they coach and empower married couples and couples preparing for marriage. They are available for speaking engagements together or individually.

Dr. Kimberly is passionate about seeing people discover their individual, God-given purpose and learn their worth. She loves to see them doing what they are called to do and finding joy in it. Kimberly's joy is to inspire, empower, and transform lives through ministry, coaching, speaking, and strong relationships. She is the founder of Women of Worth Ministry.

Dr. Kimberly and her husband reside in North Texas and have two adult children, Mychal and Victoria.

CONNECT

www.drkimberlywinters.com

info@drkimberlywinters.com

****

FOLLOW

www.facebook.com/drkimberlytransforms

www.instagram.com/drkimberlywinters

Made in the USA
Coppell, TX
26 December 2021

70119206R00046